May every passing year remind you
of the precious gift of life and
bring you the constant blessing of
family and friends.

ISBN: 978-1-68088-383-1

Printed in China.
First Printing: 2021

Blue Mountain Arts, Inc.

P.O. Box 4549, Boulder, Colorado 80306

My Wishes for you
This Christmas

☆

Marci

Blue Mountain Press ™
Boulder, Colorado

May you be blessed with all the good things in life... faith, hope, love, and the blessing of good friends. If you have these things, whatever challenges life brings, you will get through. Your faith will light your path... hope will keep you strong... the love you give to others will bring you joy... and your family and friends will remind you of what is important in life.

May You
Always
Believe
in
Miracles

Angels are sent from heaven to remind us of the gifts we have in our family and friends and to keep us focused on the opportunities we are given to experience unconditional love through the connections we make. On the day when you most need it, and least expect it, you will be blessed by the guidance of an angel and touched by God's love. Watch for your angel today!

At Christmastime, Angels Are Everywhere

Christmas is a time when we see angels everywhere. They give us hope that the days ahead will be full of joy.

They are a beautiful gift from heaven, turning this time of year into a season of giving and sharing.

They remind us of our faith and of the things that bring lasting happiness.

May You Be
Blessed With
Strength
of
Spirit

May the hand of God bless you...
guide you... provide for you... give
you hope when days are long...
give you patience when things go
wrong... fill you with joy for the
little things... and remind you that
you are always in His care.

Faith Is the
Assurance of
Things
Not
Seen

Faith
is the
way

Faith is knowing that God is always by your side through all of life's journey and guiding your steps every day. It is believing that a power greater than ourselves knows what is best for us and those around us. It is the foundation that we come to rely on as we take our journey through life.

May Prayer
Guide
Your
Path

Prayer is the way we open our hearts to God's love and receive the help that is always there for us.

Prayer is the key that unlocks the door to better understanding and acceptance.

Prayer is the path to experience the many blessings in our lives and the way we confirm our trust in God's magnificent power.

Pray and Believe

Say two prayers...
"help" and "thank you."

Give thanks for each day in advance.

Live each day one at a time.

Remember, your angel is always with you, enfolding you in God's grace.

Believe that everything is working out for your highest good.

May Hope
Keep
You
Strong

Hope is a gift from God. It is a state of mind in which we remember that our needs are always taken care of and that miracles are before us every day. Hope is a blessing we can give to others as we encourage their dreams, comfort their sorrows, and remember together that the bonds of love are everlasting.

Just When It Seems
That All Is Lost,
Hope
Blows
in
like a
Breeze

After a big storm — look for a rainbow.

Help is always there when you are ready.

You may feel that you are all alone as life brings challenges to overcome and hardships to bear. But when you least expect it, help will appear.

When a storm bends a tree to the ground, the roots become stronger.

May Love
    Be a Constant
        in
        Your
        Life

Love is a miracle. It has given poets and authors reason to write for thousands of years.
We ponder its meaning...
We seek its light...
We experience joy because of it...
We grieve at its loss...
and we stand in awe of its power.

Love, as much as we try to define it, only holds up to its definition as a verb. When we commit ourselves and say "I will," we begin to understand the mysterious, life-sustaining miracle called love.

The Love of Family
Will Get You
Through Whatever
Life
Brings

Family
Is a
Blessing

Family means having someone to give you a hug when you need one.

Family means having someone to love you through good times and bad.

Family means having someone to share life's joys and to dry the tears through life's sorrows.

May You Be
Blessed With
Lasting
Friendships

A lifetime yields only a few lasting friendships. It happens when two special people meet and connect heart and soul. There develops an understanding of what is in each other's heart that transcends words... there is a nurturing of the spirit that is mutual... there is an exchange of love and support that is essential... and there is a sense of belonging and knowing that their friendship was meant to be.

Friendship Means...

Friendship means never having to face the challenges of life alone.

Friendship means having a witness to life's tiny, special moments that are so much better when shared.

Friendship means that there is someone
who understands where you've been,
knows where you want to go, and
accepts you for who you are.

Friendship means sharing a closeness
of spirit that gives life meaning.

During This
Special Season,
I Wish
You All
This
and More

Faith · Hope · Love

That you remember to start each day with a quiet reflection so your heart is open to the grace that comes your way.

That you see each struggle as an opportunity for enlightenment and growth.

That you let go of things not meant for you and focus on the choices in life that are yours.

I Wish You
Happiness

Remember that happiness is contagious. Make someone smile and the good feelings come right back to you.

Be grateful for the little things in life that are free. Make a list and add to it each morning.

Believe that, ultimately, everything happens for a reason. Acceptance leads the way to happiness.

I Wish
You Peace

Hold positive thoughts in your
heart and be at peace...

Peace in knowing who you are.

Peace in knowing what you believe.

Peace as you look back at your life,
accepting that every step was guided.

Peace as you sleep, knowing that
your life is in the care of the angels.

I Wish
You Joy

May your dreams unfold before you and fulfill the desires of your heart.

May faith always be the light that guides your journey home.

May every passing year remind you of the precious gift of life and bring you the constant blessing of family and friends.

May You
Remember These
Things at
Christmastime...
and All
Year
Through

If you have good friends, you have almost everything.

To love and be loved... that is life's greatest gift. To share joy with those most important in your life... that is a blessing.

Every day is a gift and a reason to celebrate.

About Marci

Marci began her career by hand painting floral designs on clothing. No one was more surprised than she was when one day, in a single burst of inspiration and a completely new and different art style, her delightful characters sprang from her pen! "Their wild and crazy hair is a sign of strength," she thought, "and their crooked little smiles are endearing." She quickly identified the charming characters as Mother, Daughter, Sister, Father, Son, Friend, and so on until all the people and places in life were filled. Then, with her own loved ones in mind, she wrote a true and special sentiment to each one. This would be the beginning of a wonderful success story, which today still finds Marci writing each and every one of her verses in this same personal way.

Marci is a self-taught artist who has always enjoyed writing and art. She is thrilled to see how her delightful characters and universal messages of love have touched the hearts and lives of people everywhere. Her distinctive designs can also be found on Blue Mountain Arts greeting cards, calendars, bookmarks, and other gift items.

To learn more about Marci, look for Children of the Inner Light on Facebook or visit her website: www.MARCIonline.com.